LOL sis

'LIVE OUT LOUD'

By Wakiekie Reid

Wakiekie Reid

Po box 1530

Stockbridge, GA 30281

470-278-3047

wakiekie@reiditroup.com

INTRODUCTION

It's been said, "what don't kill us make us stronger". I would associate that quote with 'Woman'. From the start of our menstrual,the first high school breakup, childbirth or marriage,we learn to endure and find light at the end of every tunnel.

CHAPTER 1

This is my season to speak my mind, follow my heart and step out on faith. God got me

CHAPTER 2

I will no longer be bound by the things of this world. I am preparing a mental place of eternal fulfillment; Peace

CHAPTER 3

Manifest in your mood daily what your heart desires and it shall be yours. Walk, talk, and act like it's already done.

CHAPTER 4

Be joyful even when you are not happy, while emotions may change, Gods promise to give you joy remains the same. Stop letting the devil steal your joy

CHAPTER 5

Remember the things that broke you, so you always know what it takes to rebuild.

CHAPTER 6

Share your knowledge with others. Growth comes in numbers.

CHAPTER 7

Testify to the weary, your story could help someone.

CHAPTER 8

Its ok to YELL at the demons when you are alone , its necessary to discipline unruly thoughts.

CHAPTER 9

Blast your music, sing loudly, dance around to your favorite, laugh at corny jokes, silly moments are good for the soul.

CHAPTER 10

Pick up the phone and call someone you haven't spoken with in a while, don't ask for anything, just give your attention. Someone may need your silent support. Show up for someone today

CHAPTER 11

Pay it forward. Even when we think we have not enough, someone has less. All that we have comes from the Lord, share as the most high have with you.

CHAPTER 12

Cherish the people who are meaningful to you. Be a good steward of the things that are meaningful to you.

CHAPTER 13

Treat yourself often.

A date with you is good for the soul.

Enjoy your own company and you will appreciate the company

of others more.

CHAPTER 14

Fall in love with you daily.

Created with so much thought and uniqueness.

I promise you will find something new and beautiful about you every time you search.

Took me years to realize I had few freckles 😊

CHAPTER 15

Vent without complaining.

There can be no healing if we mask the damage.

Its good to let it out while finding a solution

Wound care is necessary to heal the wound.

CHAPTER 16

Acknowledge its ok to walk round bruised.

You are not broken.

Ain't no shame in our failures, bad choices/relationships

CHAPTER 17

Have Faith

That what you prayed for will happen.

Because it is!

CHAPTER 18

Live a life you are not ashamed of

Create the life you want to live until you die .

CHAPTER 19

Date until you are prepared mentally for commitment.

Don't drag others into your unstable space.

Get to know you before asking for his life story.

CHAPTER 20

Focus on the plate in front of you before asking for seconds. Complete one course at a time.

CHAPTER 21

Understand men are very different than women.

Once you have you will spare yourself the constant confusion

of trying to make him think like you.

Compliment the indifference with understanding.

CHAPTER 22

Don't be afraid to ask for HELP.

We are strong by nature but we were never made to do it all.

CHAPTER 23

Moving in silence should never require you to be ashamed to celebrate every win

Focus in silence but celebrate loud

You worked hard to achieve every milestone in your life

You deserve to have the cake and eat it too, right?

CHAPTER 24

Stop concerning yourself with others opinion of you
or trying to be anyone other than who GOD created you to
be. For the plans GOD has for you are for YOU.

FINALE

LIVE OUT LOUD SIS ....